Contents

Why should we do Crafts with Kids?

Crafts and Creative activities are proven to be helpful in EARLY LEARNING and EARLY CHILDHOOD DEVELOPMENT.

Involving kids in crafts that involve hand and finger muscle movements, coordination between hands and eyes, use of pincer grip etc. enhance –

- Fine and gross motor skills
- Cognitive skills
- Sensory skills
- Hand- eye Coordination
- Critical thinking
- Imagination

Along with the skill development in children, crafts also boost ***creative thinking*** and ***imagination*** as well as ***ability to express*** them.

A Sense of achievement and ***relaxation*** are bonus parts of indulging kids in creative activities.

Arts and Crafts are always beneficial in improving productivity and social skills as well.

Points to Remember:

- Don't guide them too much
- Give them freedom to explore and express
- Keep expectations low
- Don't force or pressurize to something if they are not in mood or don't show interest
- Repetition is key – do the same activity again if they didn't participate earlier
- Involve with them
- Be prepared to handle mess
- Keep tissues, wipe clothes handy

Happy Crafting!
Get Creative!!

Alphabet Name Spaceship

What is that one word that every child wants to write first once he learns alphabets?

OWN NAME. Right!

And once they learn the spelling of their own name, they want to write their own name all over the place.So what could be more interesting than making an Alphabet Name Spaceship for their own name, and mine was generous enough to make one for mommy too ;).

Material Required:

- Colored paper (i had colored sticker paper, so used these)
- Glue
- Scissors
- Black sheet for background
- Stars (stickers or cut from paper)

Step 1: Cut the colored paper in the shapes shown – Small rectangles, triangles, and long stripes. If the child can cut, let him try cutting simple shapes with child-safe scissors (supervision required).

Step 2: Use glue for sticking the colored paper if you are not using sticking papers in the shape of a spaceship (see pic for ref.). Using black or dark blue background/paper will give better look of space.

Let them choose the colors order for spaceship (rectangles).

Step 3: Either write alphabets before and let them stick in the order of spelling Or Use markers to write the names after sticking and allow it to dry.

Step 4: Adding stars to the space is very important ;). Use star stickers or draw and color the stars, or if you use stamps; and our **Alphabet Name Spaceships** for baby and mummy are ready.

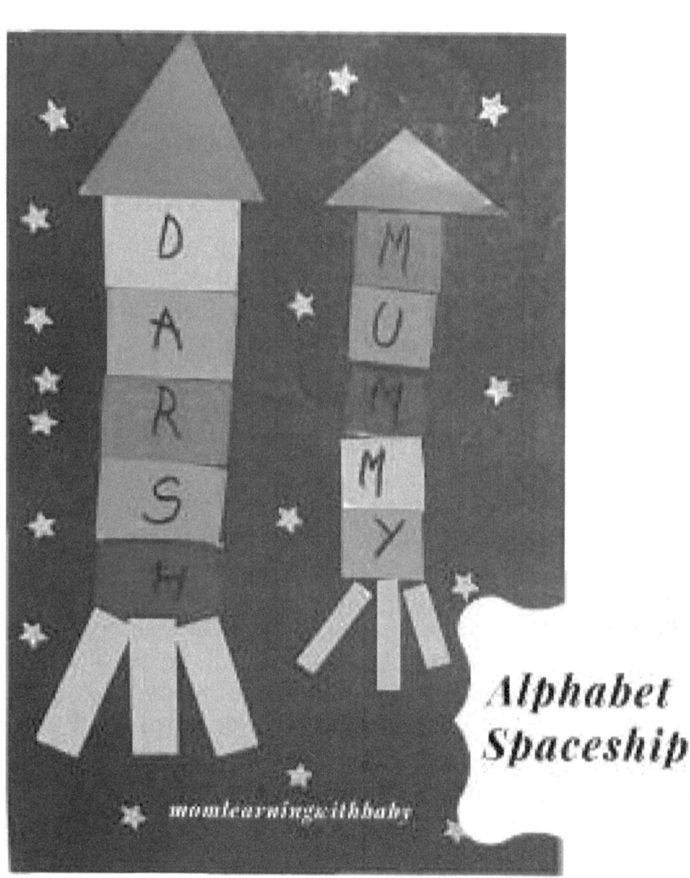
D
A
R
S
H
M
U
M
M
Y
Alphabet
Spaceship
momlearningwithbaby

Bookmarks for Kids

BOOKS are human's best friend and reading is one the best habit.

Though every parent wishes to start reading to kids as early as 6 months old, in the hope they will develop a habit; honestly, once they start getting distracted with outer world and start enjoying toys & friends more, it becomes difficult to continue the reading habit. Ofcourse some kids are born reader.

So encouraging the children to make their own BOOKMARKS and keep them in the books they read might be helpful in bringing back the interest in books and inducing a habit which they will always be thankful for.

Material Required:

- Chartpaper/ cardboard/ cereal box/ cloth tag
- Scissors
- Colors
- Googly eyes
- Stars – paper or stickers
- Glue
- Thread/ribbon

Minion Bookmark

This is a recycled craft, and it is just a 5-minute craft. It's always nice and fun to recycle waste stuff/trash. Any cloth tag or cereal box can be used by just coloring or sticking paper on it.

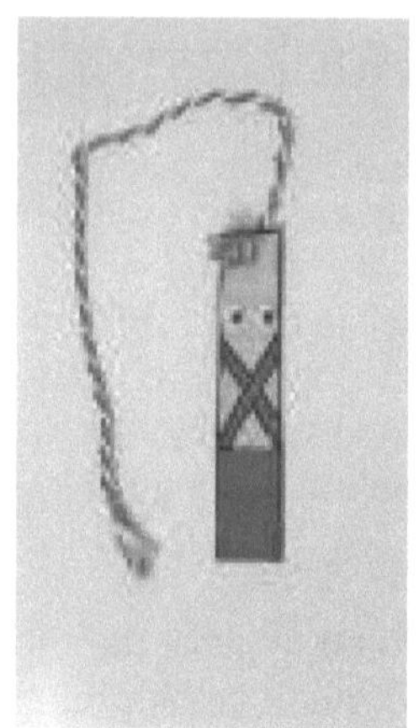

Steps:

- Cut a chartpaper/ cardboard/cereal box/cloth tag in rectangular shape
- Color it
- Adding the googly eyes gives extra fun to simple minion bookmark. Even kids can make it on their own.
- Punch hole
- For the thread, you can use ribbon or lace or simply recycle any rakhi or jwellery thread.

Starry Bookmarks

Stars make pretty bookmarks.

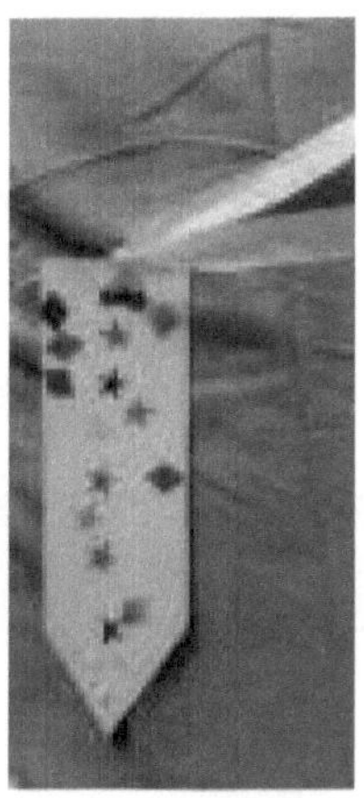

This simple and easy to make bookmark is good for keeping kids buys for sometime as well as refining their fine motor skills. Also kids love sticking anything especially stars.

Steps

- Cut a plain or colored chartsheet/ cardboard/chart paper/cereal box in any shape and size
- Stick stars or any stickers/ embellishments
- Punch hole
- Tie thread/lace

Below are 2 FREE PRINTABLE Bookmarks, just for your convenience and try these first to be sure if making creative bookmarks will work for your kid.

My Bookmarks

<h1 style="text-align:center">*My Bookmarks*</h1>

Download these 2 FREE Printable Bookmarks and encourage kids to use them while reading. They will enjoy turning pages and placing the cute owl bookmarks in their books.

- Print them and stick on sturdier cardboard- may be cereal boxes or chart paper
- Punch hole
- Tie thread/lace etc.

The owl with glasses is my favorite, isn't it cute!

Take book reading experience to another level with customized bookmarks.

Happy Reading!

Create with Clay Dough/Play dough

Clay Dough/ Play dough is one of the most versatile material. It is perfect for sensory activities and kids can have fun while creating. The clay doughs are soft and re-usable, which make them perfect buy to entertain kids.

Some more proven benefits of clay dough/play dough are:

- Strengthening finger muscles
- Enhancing fine-motor skills
- Sensory development
- Improving pre-writing skills
- Developing hand-eye coordination
- Creativity & Imagination
- Calming activity
- Free play
- Cognitive development

Material Required:

- Colorful clay dough/ play dough
- Shape cutters (optional)
- Child-safe Knife (optional)

So basically we only need colorful clay dough/play dough and create any number of things with them – like colorful caterpillar, flowers, dinosaur family, vegetables, cats, even practice writing numbers and alphabets.

Allow the child to roll, flatten, and make the shape he wants to create.

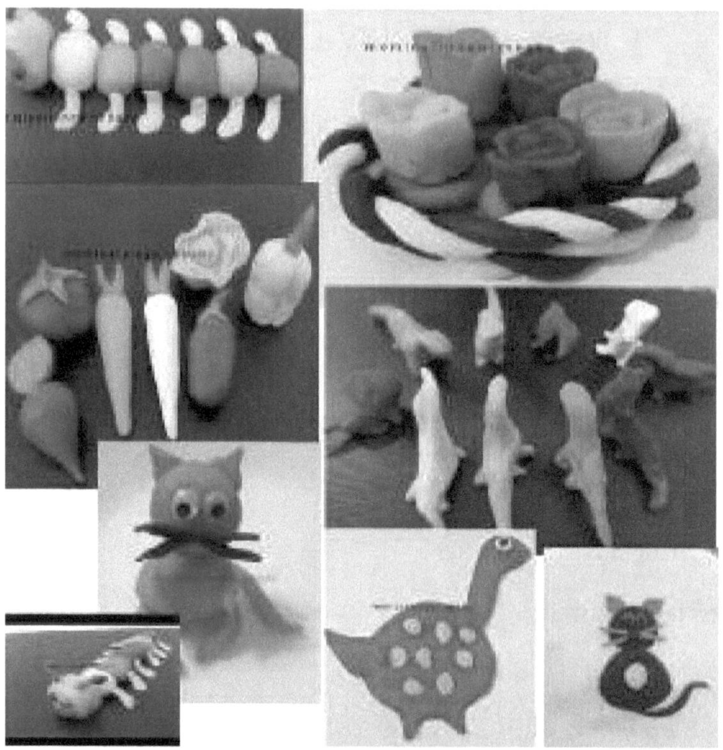

Activities:

- Learning about fruits and vegetables
- Understanding of shapes, sizes
- Recognition of animals/insects
- Writing practice of alphabets, numbers and spellings

Diwali Crafts and Activities

DIWALI or Deepawali – is the biggest Hindu festival. It refers to the festival of lights which is celebrated by lighting rows of lamps (deep or diyas). It signifies victory of truth, triumph of good over evil, knowledge over ignorance and light over darkness.

Festival of **Diwali** is celebrated in the *Kartik month* which falls around October or November, the exact dates vary every year according to the Hindu Calendar.

Decorating Diyas:

Kids love colors and what would be better than lighting the lamps decorated by the tiny hands. So just let them paint the diyas with their imagination. They can even stick stars, mirrors or embellishments to their hand-painted diyas.

Rangoli:

Draw a simple design by chalk/white color on floor and allow them to fill their colors of choice. Elder kids can draw their own rangoli designs as well.

For younger kids, rangoli can be created on chart paper or paper plate or cardboard – by applying glue over a design and then letting them spread the colors over glue.

Stories/Books:

Kids have a lot of queries and curiosity about the reasons behind rituals and practices. So it's nice to read this all to them and enlighten them through books written for kids.

Lamps/Lanterns:

Easy to make colorful paper lamps or lanterns will add beauty to the festive decor of the house.

Greeting Cards:

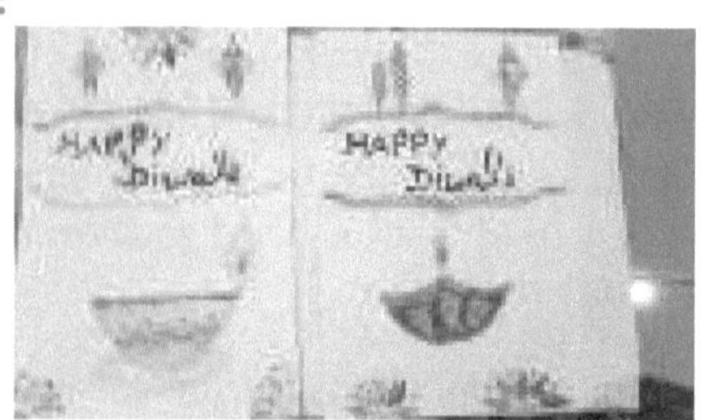

It's always lovely to give each other festive cards, and it would cherish relations by teaching kids to prepare cards for their friends, teachers and even family members.

Use glitter pens, glitter glue, foam, star stickers, etc. to decorate the card. We made these Diwali cards for teachers.
A greeting card is included in the FREE PRINTABLE (LINK BELOW)
Diwali Activity Sheets

Kandils:

Kandils are traditional part of house decor on Diwali. Make kandils with paper or by sticking colored paper on chart sheet. Decorate with stars, glitters, embellishments.

Easy Popsicle Crafts

Popsicles are multi-purpose, colorful and give superb scope to creativity. One can make anything under the sun using popsicles. Buy the colored ones or color the plain ones & color them.

Kids can make airplanes, photo frames, felt ice-creams, bookmarks, snowflakes, star, reindeer, magic wand, flags, Christmas tree etc. using popsicles or ice-cream sticks.

Learning shapes,colors and numbers using popsicles will make learning much more fun and easy to understand and remember.

Popsicle Photo Frames

We made Popsicle sticks ***memory frame*** to gift daddy on for Father's Day and a rainbow frame for a friend to gift on her birthday. These hand-made gifts are the best.

Here is a quick <u>video</u> of simple easy DIY Popsicle Photo Frames.

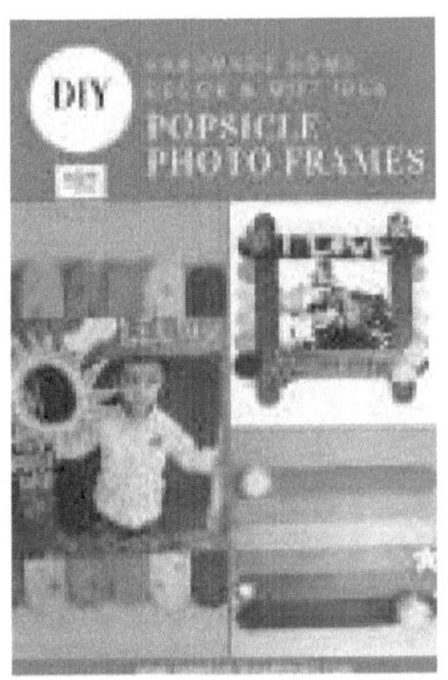

Felt Ice Creams

These *ice-cream crafts* are perfect summer craft. They allow the child to utilize imagination and let them decorate their own ice-lolly with pompoms, glitter, stars and embellishments. This activity is good for fine motor skills.

Popsicle Bookmarks

Simply stick a glittery foam or paper star or any sticker to popsicle, and use it as bookmark.

Add googly eyes to the glittery star for more fun. and it becomes magic wand too.

Popsicle Snowflakes& Stars

Make beautiful Snowflakes and stars with popsicles and decorate them with pompoms, stars or embellishments or glitters.

Please note: Let the glue dry for some time on the popsicles before starting decoration.

Fall Crafts

Fᴀʟʟ or Autumn season is the one that comes before winter, when the leaves fall from the trees, hence the name Fall Season. Because leaves change color and so the color of the season is predominantly Orange-Yellow.

The Fall Crafts mostly include dried orange leaves (mostly maple leaves), pumpkin, owl, hedge-hog, trees in the shade of orange-yellow-red leaves, apple & apple pie.

Let's make some absolutely quick & easy crafts with whatever is available at home.

Bubble Wrap Fall Tree

Who doesn't love popping those bubble wraps that come with the packaging! Oh we all do, right!

But there is a better use of it as well than just popping.. *bubble wrap tree*.

Material Required:

- Bubble wrap
- Paints- orange, yellow, brown
- Brush
- White paper

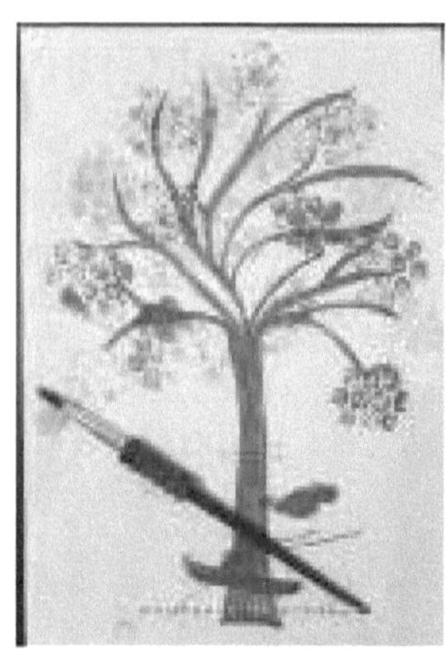

Step 1: Draw and color tree on white paper
Step 2: Color leaves using bubble wrap with orange-yellow-red colors
There can be multiple variations in this art depending on whether you want to apply color to bubble wrap with brush and then put it on paper (pic 1 above) or just dip bubble wrap in color(s) and dab on paper (pic 2 below).

Mixing and overlapping yellow and orange make perfect fall leaves.

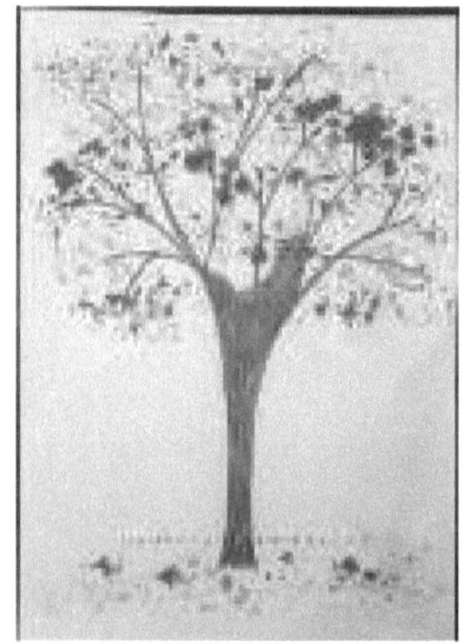

Pointillism Fall Tree

Pointillism art is created by using a q-tip or ear buds, as we call them. Basically painting by a point.

This _Pointillism art_ has multiple benefits including fine motor skills, neural development and is purely therapeutic & calming.

Material Required:

- q-tip – 1 or more (tied with rubber band or thread)
- Paint – yellow and orange, brown
- Plain paper

Step 1: Draw tree with brown color
Step 2: Dip q-tip in colors and dab on tree branches

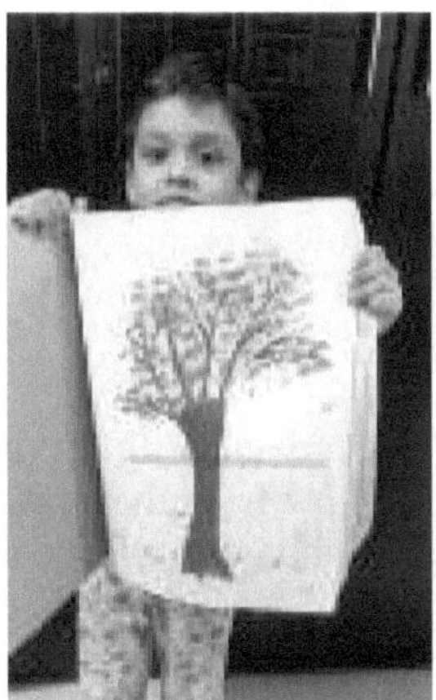

Paper Plate Pumpkin

One of the most favorite fall craft is paper plate pumpkin or paper pumpkin, and there can be so many versions of it- stick or color black eyes and mouth or cut the paper for eyes and make a pumpkin mask or stick paper plate pumpkin on a popsicle.

Make a crown by sewing or sticking orange colored paper leaves or real leaves, if you have, on a head band or any cloth/paper strip and tie/sew/stick as a crown.

Like I made the fall-leaf crown, similarly fall-leaf wreath can be made by cutting leaves from orange colored paper and sticking to a wreath or ribbon or cardboard.

Fall Tree by Blowing Paint

This activity was super fun and is a bit tricky as well. The consistency of the pint is very important along with the direction of blowing.

Material Required:

- Plain paper
- Colors – diluted yellow & orange, brown
- Straw
- Brush

Steps: Drop colors (not too diluted) on the paper with the brush or dropper and tell the child to blow from the straw. Just need to explain to the child the direction from which the air should be blown so that the paint flows in opposite direction.

The mixing of yellow and orange gives perfect fall tree appearance.

Greeting Card for Teacher

Greeting Cards are the best way to show gratitude and respect and care towards a person who teaches us lessons of life especially on the occasion of Teacher's Day.

Well the greeting cards are always perfect for birthdays, occasions, festivals, new year to give to friends, family, relatives, neighbors and parents, of course. Everyone appreciates and cherishes the hand-made cards, these strengthen love and bonding.

Flower Vase Greeting Card for Teachers – which kids can make on their own:

The technique we are using here is called **Pointillism**, except we are using a bunch of q-tips instead of single one.

We chose a flower vase. You can make a bouquet of colorful flowers as well.

Material Required:

- Colored paper – any color, any paper
- q-tips (4-5)
- Rubber band
- Red & green water color
- Brush
- Plain paper
- Glitter glue (optional)

Step 1: Cut the plain paper (white preferably) in the shape and size of the greeting card.

Step 2: Cut the colored paper (i have taken red crepe paper), in the shape of a flower vase and stick on the plain paper (cut in the shape of greeting card).

Step 3: Paint the stems with green color (sketch pens, water colors, crayons) from the vase to the top

Step 4: Tie 4-5 q-tips with rubber band tightly so they don't fall off while coloring

Step 5: Dip the q-tips in the red color (don't add water in color, keep thick consistency) and dab on the paper on the edges of the green stems

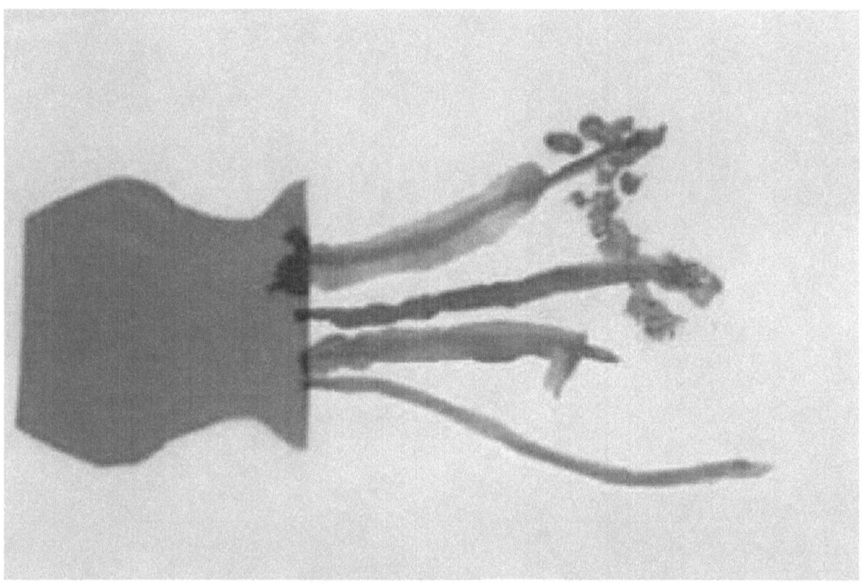

Step 6: Repeat the step 5 to cover all the green stems with red flowers. A little overlapping on the stem is fine, just don't make too many red flowers.

Add glitters glue on the card for added sparkle, who doesn't love glitters anyways!

Make pretty colorful greeting cards for teachers, parents, friends and make them happy. Encourage the child to Write a beautiful message inside - let the child write his name /message on his own.

GREETING CARD
FOR TEACHERS

www.momlearningwithbaby.com

Happy Birthday Marbled Card

Birthdays are always special and can be made more special by a hand-made cards or gifts. Let's try a different type of greeting card - with marbled paper.

Here is an interesting experiment with Shaving Foam & Food colors – *Clouds & Rain*.

You need to see and perform this shaving foam experiment to understand how this marbled pattern was formed (click here). Learning is always more fun with easy experiments.

Material Required:

- Shaving foam
- Food colors
- Glass jar
- Water
- Dropper
- Thick white chart paper (small piece)

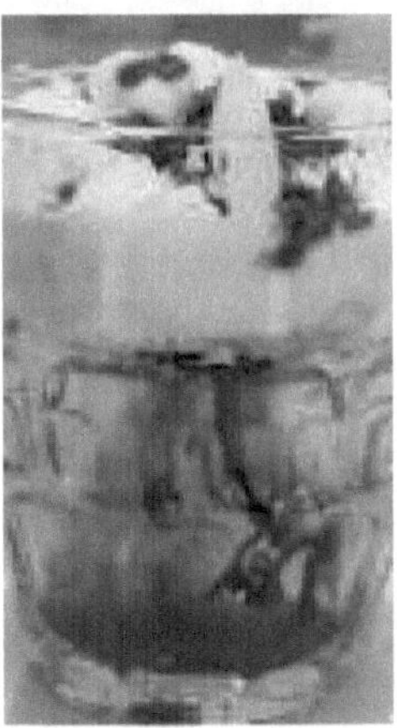

After you have done the experiment, you need to quickly make a marbled paper.

How to make marbled paper?

Step 1: Now Once we are done with the experiment and enjoyed the penetration or rain of colors though shaving foam clouds in the glass jar, just mix the colors on the foam with a pointed knife of fork.

The thick layer of shaving foam has colors on the upper side and the foam is till the edge of the jar. So i just made a pattern sort of by gently mixing the colors with a fork – in a zig-zag way.

You know you can actually make this marble pattern on a paper without the whole experiment as well, but then it will be just marbling of paper, and adding it up with the shaving foam experiment, it's two-in-one – science experiment and craft. Plus, kid can enjoy some messy play once you are done marbling the papers.

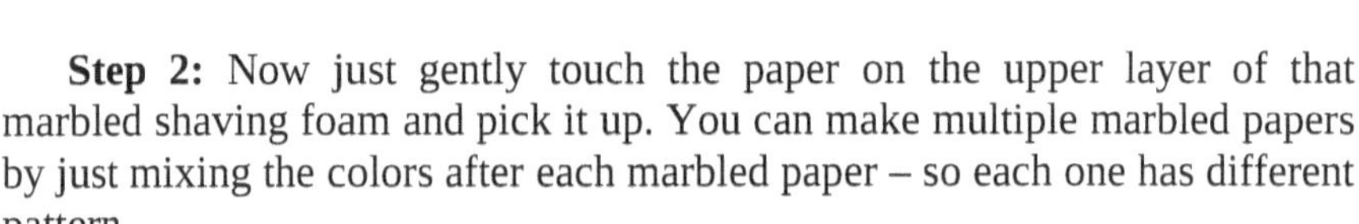

Step 2: Now just gently touch the paper on the upper layer of that marbled shaving foam and pick it up. You can make multiple marbled papers by just mixing the colors after each marbled paper – so each one has different pattern.

Step 3: Scrape off the extra foam gently with a knife or fork by keeping the paper on another surface.

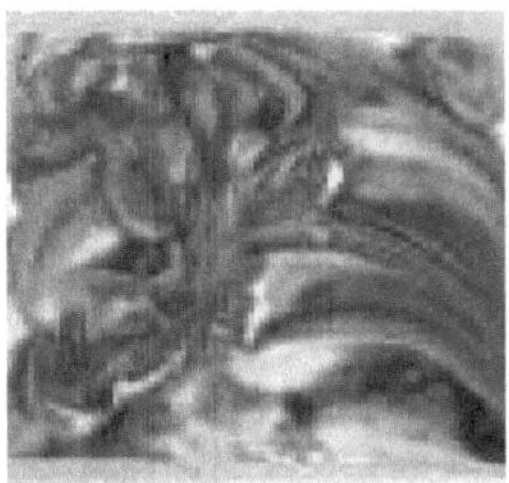

Step 4: Let it dry completely. Takes time. Don't rush. The outcome is going to be gorgeous when it's dried.

NOTE: The size of paper I took was just the one that can sit on the edge of my jar. Keep that in mind while cutting the chartpaper.

Step 6: Cut the marbled paper in the shape of heart or any desired shape and stick on white/ any color paper. Draw hearts/ flowers/ stars as per child's wish and write beautiful personalized message.
Encourage the child to do all the steps, as per his/her ability.

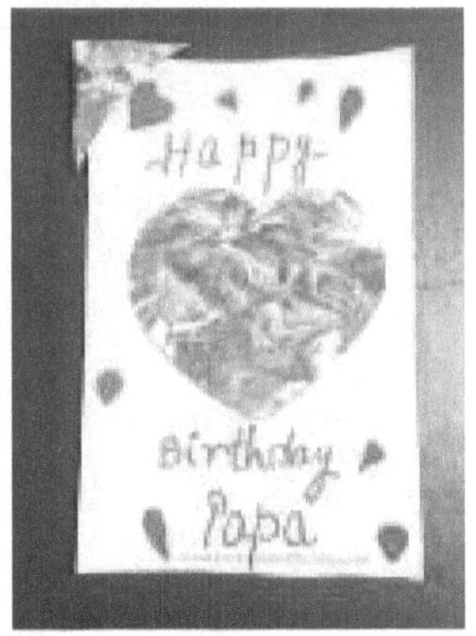

Also Read: 50+ Father's Day Hand-made Gifts

Indian Flag Crafts

TIRANGA or Tricolor, the Indian Flag, the name is enough to fill us with the proud feeling. Every Indian citizen must know the details of the Tiranga- it's 4 colors and the Ashoka Chakra.

Indian Independence day, 14th August, and Republic Day, 26th January are the most common occasions where we indulge in hoisting Indian Flag Crafts every year in schools, colleges, public places, government institutes etc.

Such occasions are the best time to teach kids about our country's history and glorious past and how our brave warriors have earned Independence for us and why we must learn to value it, respect it and use it wisely.

Making Flag crafts with kids is the best way to introuce Tiranga to them and help them learn about their history.

Paper Cone Wreath Tiranga

A simple and easy wreath made with colorful paper cones arranged in the color pattern of Tricolor.

Material Required:

- Colored papers – orange, white and green
- Glue
- Cardboard
- Scissors
- Ruler
- Pencil
- Blue colored foam or paper

It is easy to make out from the picture below that it's a simple craft made by sticking ornage, white and green paper cones in the correct tri-color order on cardboard.

Check the step by step tutorial of Paper Cone Tiranga Craft here.

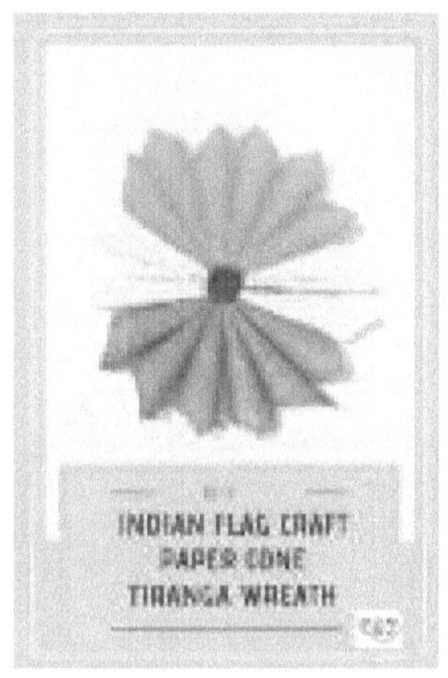

Young kids might need assistance in cutting the same size papers, making cones and sticking them in order on cardboard.

The main aim of making flag crafts is to make child aware of the colors and color pattern of the flag and.

Don't forget to play some patriotic songs and National Anthem.

Few **more easy Tiranga crafts** to make with kids are:

1. Popsicle Flag
2. Handprint Flag
3. Tiranga with grains/pulses
4. Pompom flag

Jellyfish Swimming Craft

J for Jellyfish – don't we all love the pretty umbrella-shaped marine animal floating with its tentacles. A collection if jellyfish is called "bloom", "smack" or "swarm".

Jellyfish is not a fish

Though these are called Jellyfish, they aren't actually a type of fish. Fish are vertebrates, however the jellyfish are invertebrates. Their bodies constitute of *95% water* and only 5% of proteins, muscles and nerve cells.

Inspite of the beauty of jellyfish, they can be pretty dangerous if they sting any human and they paralyze their prey before eating.

Jellyfish don't have brain, heart or eyes

If you are following our journey or our blog, you would know how much we love paper plates and paper plate crafts, so here is another one of our popular crafts.

Material Required:

- Paper plate
- Felt/ chartpaper/ cardboard
- Popsicle
- Colorful yarn / thick threads/ ribbons
- Blue paint
- Markers
- Scissors
- Paper cutter/ knife
- Glue
- Googly eyes
- Green paper (optional)

Step 1: Paint the centre of the upper side of paper plate (the side we eat on) with blue color. Let it dry properly

Step 2: Cut 2 pieces of felt/chart paper of any color in the shape of umbrella or a cardboard. If you are using cardboard or white chartpaper, then color them

{I used felt as I just love the felt crafts and it becomes more sturdy}

Step 3: Stick the colorful yarn/thread strands on 1 side of a piece of umbrella shape – at the bottom (ref pic below) – don't stick too many yarns

The kids can help in sticking thje yarns on the jellyfish part.

Step 4: Stick the other piece over the piece with yarn stuck on it. (keeping the yarns in between). Let it dry properly else yarns will fall off Trim the yarns and make then even sized. Don't take very long strands.

Step 5: Stick popsicle of any color on any side of the felt/paper jelly fish. Let it dry

Step 6: Stick googly eyes on the other side (backside of popsicle side) and draw smiling face of our jellyfish using marker

Step 7: Cut the paper plate with paper cutter at a side for popsicle to slide through it (ref. pic for ref.)

Step 8: Draw stones and bubbles with black marker/paint for added ocean effect – optional

Step 9: Stick weeds /grass / plants cut out from green paper or paint – totally optional

Step 10: Insert the popsicle inside the cut we made in step 7, so that the jellyfish stays in front and popsicle goes behind and easy to move now.

Step 11: Now simply slide the jellyfish and enjoy the floating movement or the swimming jellyfish.

You can make octopus in similay way - just cut whole octopus with legs out of felt/paper.

Jelly Fish
Swimming in Ocean

www.momlearningwithbaby.com

Burj Khalifa with Wax Resist Technique

Coloring with different types of colors to create an awesome look is the art of MIXED COLOR PAINTING.

One of the type is **WAX RESIST**. This type of art is very easy to create with little kids and so very addictive at the same time. There are different techniques of Wax Resist also, few of which I will demonstrate in this post.

We are painting the iconic Burj Khalifa with Dubai skyline.

Material Required:

- Plain thick white paper
- Black Wax crayon
- Water colors – yellow, orange
- Brush
- Water

Step 1: Draw any desired pattern with either matching wax crayon on the paper – white on white, yellow on yellow, black on black – or opposite color as per your desired output. Here we drew outline of buildings and filled them with black crayon

Step 2: Step 2: Dilute the water colors and swipe with brush on the paper.

The child does not need to worry about color overlapping the building, because water color will not cover the crayon.

So child can freely paint the diluter water color over the paper.

The best part of this technique is diluted water color doesn't disturb the wax details, so even if the brush strokes go over it, it won't effect the black crayon part.

Learning Alphabets with Crafts

Learning Alphabets by doing crafts is an effective learning process for preschoolers and they understand the shapes better. Involving kids in crafts at a younger age has proven benefits on mental and cognitive development of children.

Alphabet song is the most loved rhyme of kindergarten kids. Including crafts to learn alphabets is one of the best methods to help kids remember the words associated with letters.

Using easy craft ideas which help enhance creativity and fine motor skills along with overall brain development.

Learning Alphabets, numbers or words with crafting activities is a part of montessori method of learning and has multiple benefits including imagination enhancement and cognitive development.

Few **Crafts for Learning Alphabets**

- Clay Dough
- Finger paint
- Pointillism
- PomPom alphabet
- Yarn alphabet
- Dot markers
- Mosaic Craft
- Pattern coloring

Clay Dough Alphabets

Working with Clay dough enhances fine motor skills and finger muscles along with imagination and social skills. Hand-eye coordination is increased when kids focus on the detailing. Rolling and cutting clay dough strengthens finger and hand muscles as well.

Pointillism

The <u>Pointillism</u> is an art by a tip or point. There are benefits of this technology like hand-eye coordination and focus and concentration. When the child fills the space by dipping q-tip with paint, it refines fine motor skills. This technique can be used to write alphabets or numbers.

PomPom Alphabets

Who doesn't love colorful Pompoms and decorating the kid's room with their initials decorated with colorful Pompoms would be wonderful. Using cloth pegs to stick PomPom is advanced version to strengthen finger muscles and improve hand-eye coordination.

For creating PomPom alphabets, better to use thick cardboard for cutting alphabet shapes so that it doesn't tear up because of the weight. This is a wonderful Montessori learning activity for pre-schooler kids.

Finger painting

Painting with the fingers using child-safe paints is excellent way to boost creativity and fine motor and sensory skills. Kids just love to use their fingers to explore textures and painting with fingers is a wonderful opportunity.

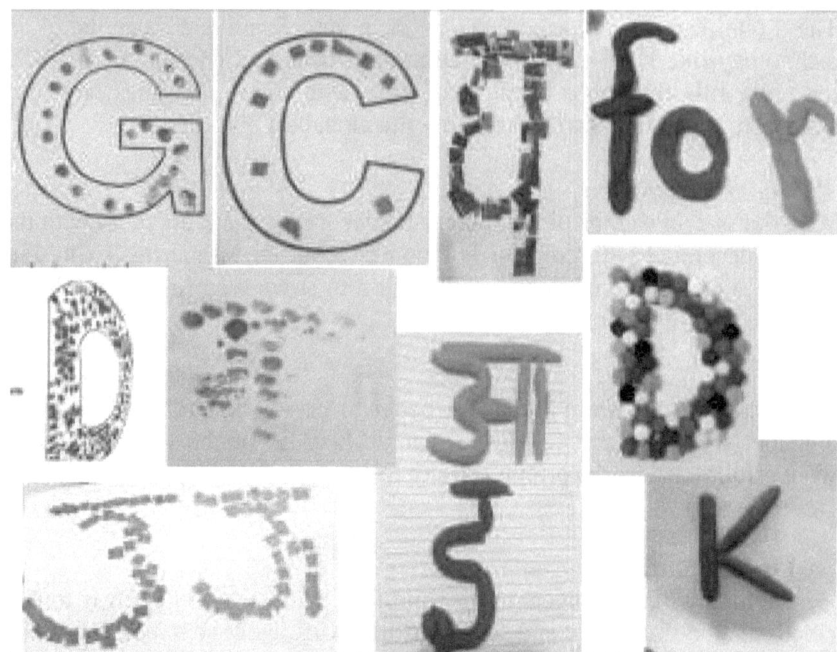

Mosaic Crafts

What is Mosaic Crafts?

A **mosaic** is a picture or design or art work made by assembling small pieces of any material like paper, foam, glass, wood etc. of similar or different colors.
Mosaic art is created by making a bigger picture with smaller pieces combined together. It can be based on a theme/ shape or just abstract.

Mosaic Craft is a very good way to work on the *fine motor skills and enhance imagination plus creating memories with kids*.

We can ask kids what they would like to create and the color theme they have in mind, giving way to their creativity is very important.

This art form can be used in simplest form to create crafts with kids which will develop their fine motor skills.

Material Required:

- Plain paper/ cardboard/ chart paper
- Colored paper – plain or textured
- Glue
- Scissors

Step 1: Draw an outline or design – start with a simple design like a traffic light or heart or car or butterfly or just any shape with not much detailing.

Step 2: Cut colored paper in small pieces (not necessarily square shape or all in equal size)

Step 3: Hand-over the drawing, glue and colored paper bits to child and let him/ her stick them as per his/ her wish. Don't instruct them much; just give them a little idea on what to do and how to do.

All the finger muscles get to work when the kid picks up the tiny piece of paper, refining pincer grip and then works on hand-eye coordination when sticking them within the boundaries.
We can also use or re-use **wrapping papers** instad of plain colored papers and recycle them to create a multicolor mosaic crafted boat or just anything.

Here I have used gift wrapping paper which I had saved from birthday party so that I can recycle them with interesting crafts. Also the 2 papers in boat below have different textures – red one is simple paper whereas blue one is thin shiny polytheism type paper. So it will count as **sensory activity** as well.

With mosaic craft/art technique, either we can make abstract designs or some particular shapes even teach alphabets and numbers to pre-schoolers.

The kids who can handle scissors can be allowed to cut paper as well.

- Alphabets – English /Hindi /any language
- Numbers
- Country Flags
- Rainbow
- Nature scenes

This type of art form can also be used to learn alphabets and numbers. Just sticking paper bits inside the outline is important not the shape or pattern of sticking it. This enhances ***hand-eye coordination and concept of boundaries as well as shapes.***

No Sew Teddy Bear

Who doesn't love a cuddly teddy bear!

How about making our own teddy bear at home in 10 minutes from a hand towel?

So here is an easy Peasy method of making a teddy bear in which kids can take part too and you don't even much supplies or skills for it. It's a no-sew teddy bear.
The **benefit** of making a teddy bear with hand towel is that –

- No risk of suffocating
- Wash it anytime
- Make a teddy bear of any color or size
- Baby can sleep with it too
- No worry of fine dust or particles for younger babies
- Dismantle and use the towel when the baby is bored of it
- No wastage

Convinced by the above listed benefits? So let's get started to make our cuddly teddy.

Material Required:

- Hand towel – any size, any color, any design
- Rubber bands
- Ribbon
- Googly eyes (optional)

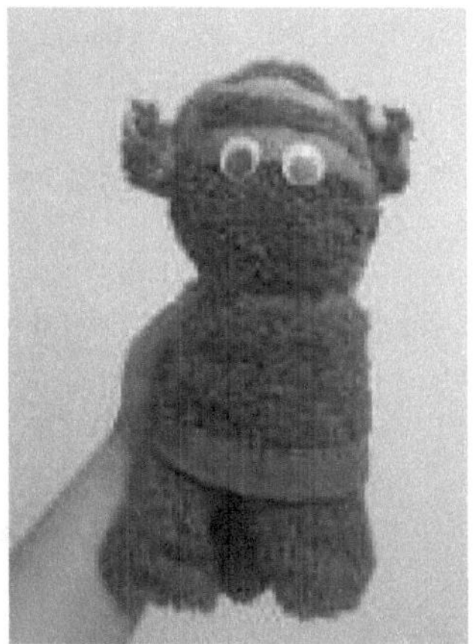

Step 1: Lay the towel flat on a surface

Step 2: Take an idea of the center of the towel and Fold one (Shorter) end till the middle of the towel

Step 3: Start rolling/ folding from the longer side till the center of the towel like making a pipe

Step 4: Repeat step 3 from the other longer side, fold till the middle. Now both sides are rolled till center and it looks like 2 pipes together

Step 5: Turn it upside down, keeping rolled sides face down

Step 6: Twist half of the roll upwards (towards left as opening it up), from the side with folded end inside (side folded in step 2)

Step 7: Turn the other end backwards from the middle, rolling it over the other already half folded side (reducing length of pipes to half)

Step 8: Open it up from corners and wrap backwards, you will see ears forming on upper side (folded end)

Step 9: Tie a rubber band from folded side, so as to secure face

Step 10: Smoothen out the front body crease and Tie rubber bands on sides for ears

Step 11: The Back side might still have foldings, but the front looks neat teddy bear shaped

Step 12: Tie ribbon over the neck rubber band and stick googly eyes on its face. Stick buttons too (totally optional).

Following the written instructions can be difficult, so here is a *video* tutorial.

Did you like the easy no-sew teddy bear?

Tissue Roll Octopus Craft

O for Octopus!

The best way to enable a child learn more words starting with same alphabet is by including a craft work in the learning process, and it makes much easier for the kid to remember.

Like it's said – *"you hear you forget, you see you remember, you make and you never forget again"*.

So most of the nurseries and homeschooling parents involve kids in more and more crafting rather than just repeating and cramming, which has definitely proved to be more beneficial.

Added benefits of doing crafts with young kids are enhancement of *fine and gross motor skills*, strengthening of *finger muscles, sensory and cognitive brain development*, to mention a few.

I am a firm believer of Recycle and Reuse, especially when it comes to crafts, diy projects and activities that we do at home. And I hoard tissue rolls, tissue boxes, cereal boxes, any kind of cardboard boxes, plastic bottles etc.

Similarly, here we will make an Octopus with a tissue roll in just 10 minutes. Easy right! So let's roll.

Tissue Roll Octopus Craft

Material Required:

- Tissue roll
- Color or colored paper
- Scissors
- Googly eyes
- Glitter glue
- Embellishments/ jewels (optional)

Step 1: Color the tissue roll with water colors/ acrylic colors or stick any colored paper. I have used blue water color. Let it dry

Step 2: Cut this stripes from one end about an inch long and few cams wide, to make the tentacles of octopus and bend them outwards. Refer pic. (cut length and width depending on the size of the tissue roll you are using)

Step 3: Stick googly eyes and paint a smile.

Step 4: Add glitter glue, embellishments or jewels – purely decorative purpose.

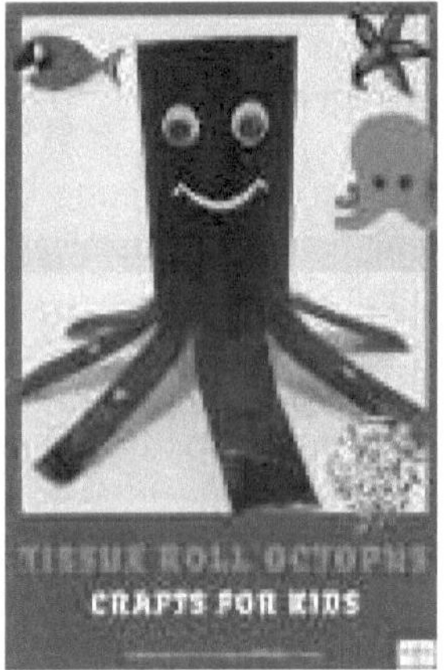

Easy peasy right? And cute too !

So don't throw away those tissue rolls or any kind of cardboard rolls or boxes you come across and you can check some ***recycling diy Crafts*** here.

We made this Octopus Craft for a recycle project in nursery. I never believed in making projects which kids can't get involve into. So always choose the easier ones for tiny kids.

Paper Plate Crafts

PAPER PLATES are my favorite craft items as the possibilities to create are endless. We just need paper plate and colors and can make literally anything we want.

So far we have made paper plate lion & dino masks, elephant & owl Craft, swimming jellyfish Craft, Gift for Dino daddy and Dino mommy, wax art, pointillism, face Craft, Pumpkin, fish, Tiranga Craft, pizza, ocean etc.
Paper plates are handy in learning concepts like - day & night, underground vegetables, food plate etc.

I always suggest parents with small kids, to keep a stock of few *essential craft supplies*, get a FREE PRINTABLE check-list here. It becomes easier to engage them in crafts and activities at home, especially in times like today, if we have stock of some of the basic craft items at home.

Kids, in general, love animals and dinosaurs and we can make face masks of any animal with just paper plate, color and googly eyes; and tie a thread or yarn from both sides of plate.

Material Required:

- Paper plates
- Child-safe colors
- Brush
- Googly eyes
- Scissors
- Glue
- Marker
- Ribbon (for face mask)
- Popsicle
- Glitter Glue (optional)

Paper Plate Dinosaur Crafts

Step 1: Cut the dinosaur shapes from a paper plate

Step 2: Let the child color the dino with colors of his/ her choice

Step 3: Cut, color and stick the spikes, head, legs and tail from the rest of the cut part of the paper plate or another paper plate (i mostly use the reaming part of the first plate)

Step 4: You can also make it a mosaic craft by sticking small pieces of colored paper over it

Step 5: Draw eyes and mouth with marker

For coloring paper plates, crayons or pencil colors or water colors can be used, as per child's age and choice.

Paper Plate Pizza:
Simply cut colorful paper pieces in circle, triangle, oval and square

shapes; and stick on a paper plate. The child can color the paper plate as well to represent pizza sauce.

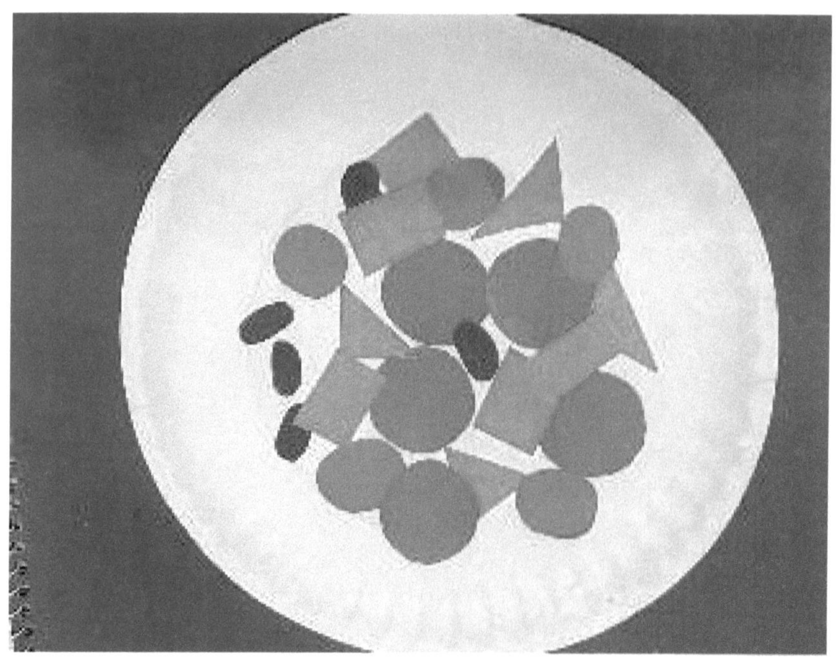

So the child learnt shapes and colors in this craft.
Tempting! Is it!
Few more paper plate crafts ideas are given below:

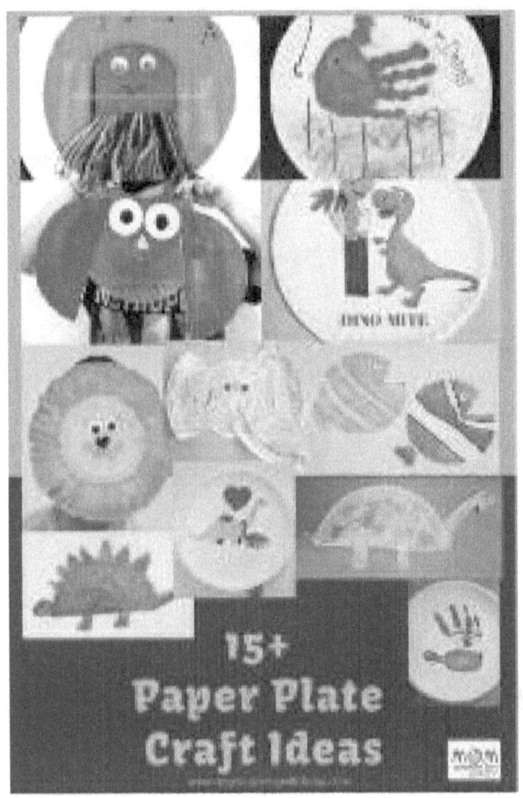#

- Lion
- Pizza
- Fish
- Owl
- Elephant
- Faces
- Food Plate
- Season cycle
- Cat/ Rabbit

No Sew Quiet Book

QUIET BOOKS are best activity books for young kids – no choking hazards, no plastics, no tearing of books; instead lots of fun and sensory skill development.

Benefits of introducing young kids to felt quiet book are:

- Enhancement of fine motor skills
- Hand-eye coordination
- Sensory skills
- Cognitive skills
- Understanding of concepts – shapes, numbers, lengths, day & night, nature, movements
- Logical reasoning

No-Sew Felt quiet books are easy to make at home, just need to have concepts in mind and replicate it.

Material Required:

- Felt sheets of different colors
- Sharp Scissors
- Hot glue
- Velcro
- Pencil/marker
- Threads/ribbons
- Thread & needle

SURPRISE EGGS – concept of hidden objects

Remember the poem "surprise eggs"? Yes, got this idea from that poem, since my toddler used to say "surprise" a lot.

Step 1: Cut felt pieces of different colors in egg shape. Cut from middle (refer pic) - 2 parts of egg

Step 2: Stick only the edges of the egg at the narrow side on the base sheet, leaving a pocket in center

Step 3: Cut any object shapes from different felt sheets – car, star, fish, bird, duck, apple etc.

Step 4: Hide the shape in each egg pocket (hidden with the upper flap) and let the exploring fun begin.

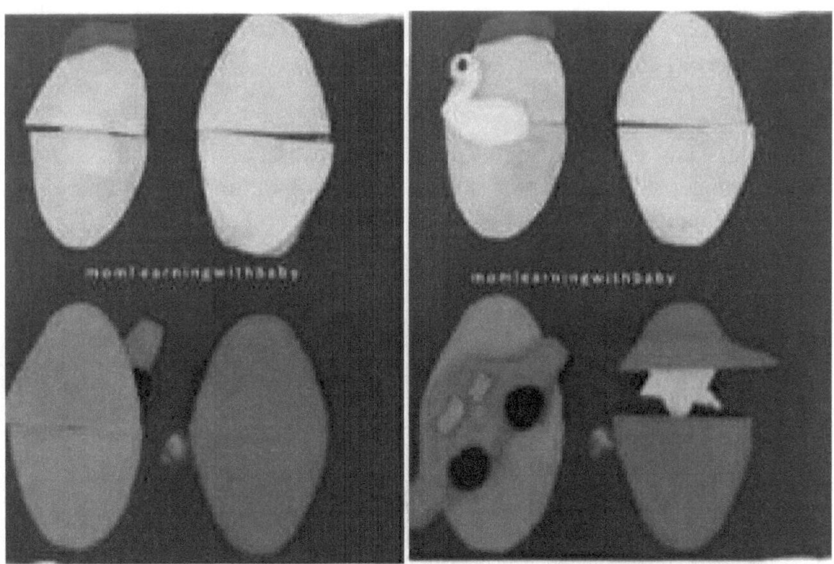

CONCEPT OF DAY & NIGHT

Step 1: Cut the shapes of house and grass with colors of choice and stick on base sheet

Step 2: Cut a square piece (smaller than base, but enough big to stick sun and clouds) of light blue color felt and stick only the 3 sides of it, above the house, leaving a pocket at the top (refer pic)

Step 3: Cut a black piece of same size of light blue felt and stick the top of it, over the edge of light blue felt, leaving the rest of black felt to be able to open as a flap (refer pic 2)

Step 4: Cut details like sun, moon, clouds, stars

Step 5: The sun, moon, clouds and stars can be stored in the pocket of light blue felt. I did not stick them or used Velcro here

Step 6: Now we have 2 scenes – a day (light blue felt) and a night (black felt) on the same page

Step 7: The child can be taught the sun and clouds are seen during day (light blue felt) and moon and stars come at night (black felt)

Isn't it easy and interesting! And so many learnings in just 1 page – logical, conceptual, fine motor skills when taking out the sun and moon from the pocket and placing over sheet and then putting them back.

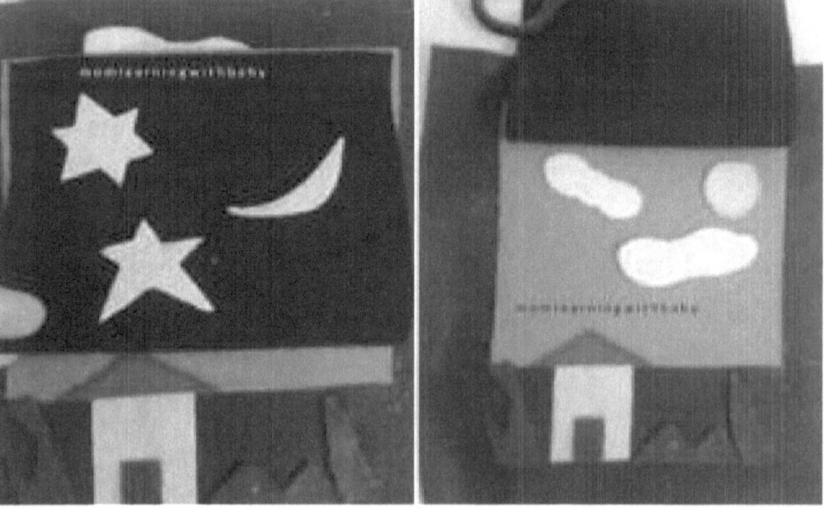

UNDERWATER THEME
Step 1: Cut sea waves with blue felt. I took 2 colors because I had, single

color is fine too

Step 2: I have hand-sewed the edges, you may stick with hot glue too, leaving the center part open as a pocket for fish & sea animals to swim

Step 3: Cut shapes of fish of other sea animals with colorful felt. Fish in the pic are market- bought

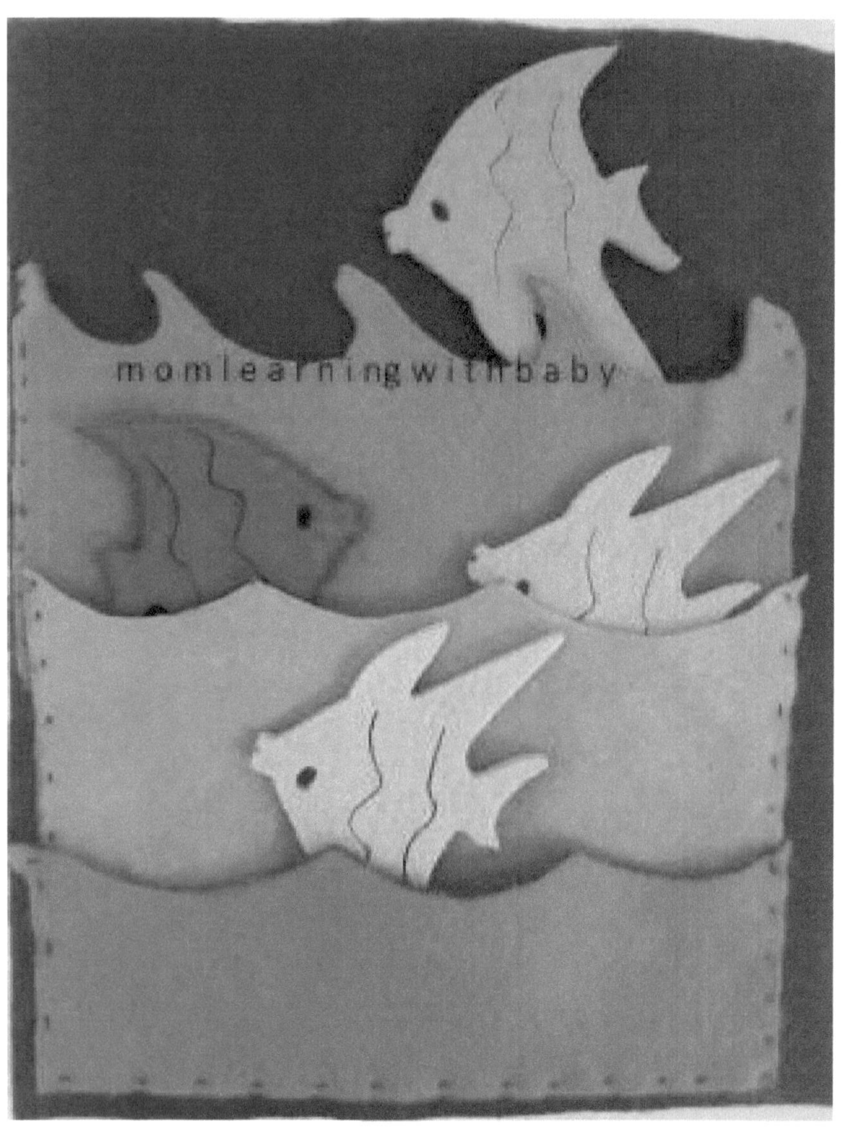

Few more concepts can be made with felt crafts are:
1. Numbers

2. Colors
3. Shapes
4. Movements
5. Fruits and vegetables
6. Time
7. Chores

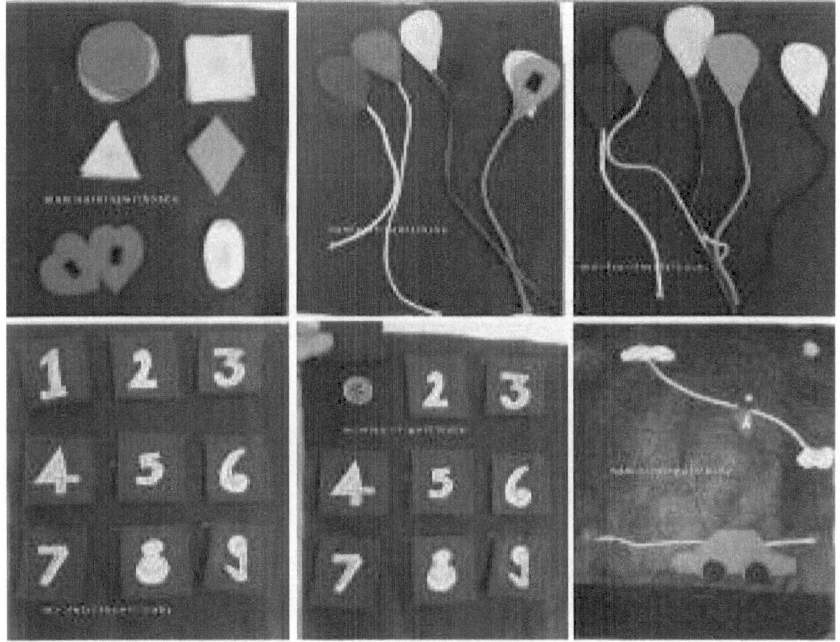

Video Tutorial 1

Video Tutorial 2

Also read more ideas of **No Sew Quiet Book.**

Recycle Trash into Crafts

Recycled & Reused Crafts are my favorite DIY projects. Always prefer up-cycling trash or recycling waste materials into interesting crafts.
 Why waste or throw when you can DIY?

It's always beneficial to start teaching kids early about going #ecofriendly and avoiding wasting and limiting use of plastic. And the kids get a message and a learning – save mother-earth.

When we must limit usage of single-use plastic and any kind of plastics overall, we all tend to fall in the trap as more than 90% of the worldly items are plastic theses days.

And picking up a water or cold-drink bottle on-the-go becomes inevitable at times. So in case, you had to buy any, why throw, just DIY and reuse or better upcycle, as these plastic bottles can't be used for storing food items or drinks.

Recycle Plastic Bottle into Police Car

Material Required:

- Plastic bottle
- Colored Chart paper for car
- Kite paper or any thinner paper of contrast color
- Black color/paint/paper
- Cardboard/ cereal box
- Scissors
- Marker
- Glue
- Paper cutter
- Star sticker (optional)

Step 1: Wrap colored paper of your choice around the bottle. We chose red

Step 2: Cut cardboard in the shape of 4 circular wheels and 1 piece for back side of the car.

Step 3: Cut a piece from the top of the car from 3 sides using paper cutter but don't remove it and pull it up. It's the seat for our policeman

Step 4: Color or stick black paper on wheels and Stick the wheels on the side

Step 5: Color or stick paper of same color (red here) of car on the circular piece we had cut in Step 2 and stick it at the back

Step 6: Cut a stripe of color contrast to the color of the car and stick at the front of the bottle (refer pic).
We chose yellow

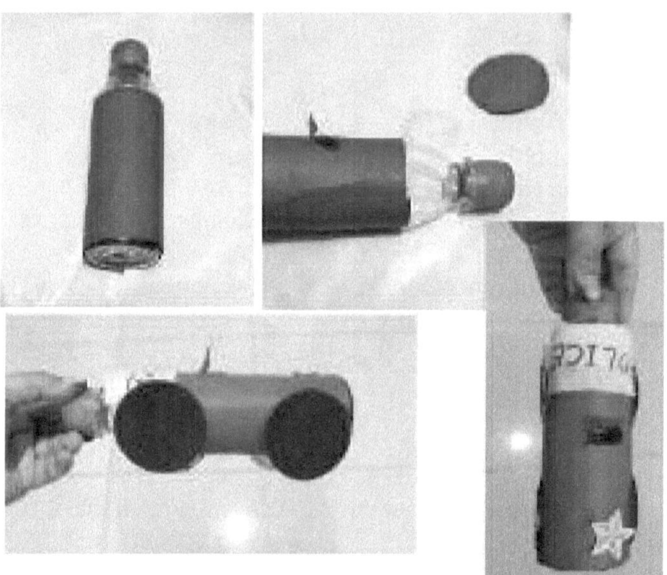

Step 7: Write POLICE in the stripe (yellow here) with a marker. Let it dry

    Step 8: Let it dry for sometime so that the wheels become firm, before handing over to the kid. Then the baby can stick stars on the car.. totally optional step.

And our Police Car is ready to roll!

Cost: ZERO!!

Do you want to see it in motion? Click *Here* !!

The same way can be used to make a racing car or just a family car also.

Material Required:

- 2 Cardboard boxes – I used a thick sturdy delivery box for fire truck and a cereal box for wheels.
- Red and Yellow colored sheets
- Scissors, marker and Glue
- Bottle cap as Alarm
- And a thread as water hose.

Looks cute, isn't it! Upcycled craft is Excellent for pretend plays and understanding of community workers. Best way to reuse tissue boxes or delivery boxes.

Let's take a look at the steps of Cardboard Fire Engine.

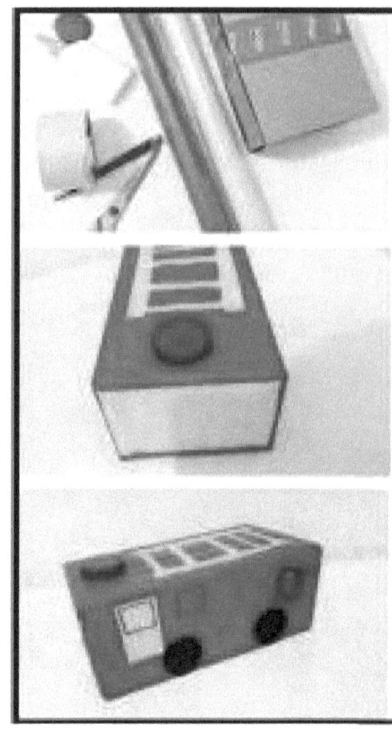

Our easy recycled cardboard Fire Engine Craft is ready!!

Similar way, you can make **Ambulance or School Bus**.

Summer Crafts & Activities

SUMMERS are approaching, though people have already lost count of days and month being home stuck and everyday is same when you work from home in pajamas and kids study from home in pajamas.

What is the best part of the summers?
One can play with water and ice and eat lots of ice cream, isn't it!
Let's make some sumer crafts.

Felt Ice-cream Craft

Every child will love decorating his/her own popsicles/lollies and it was easier to make these no-sew felt ice creams.
Material Required:

- Felt sheets of any color
- Popsicle sticks
- Scissors
- Glue
- PomPom, jewels, glitter glue, confetti – anything to decorate the popsicles

Step 1: Cut felt sheet in the shape of popsicles – 2 pieces of each color. We made 3 popsicles.

Step 2: Stick these together with popsicle sticks in between. Let it dry.

Step 3: Let the child decorate his popsicles. We used Pompoms, glitter glue and jewels/stars/embellishments.

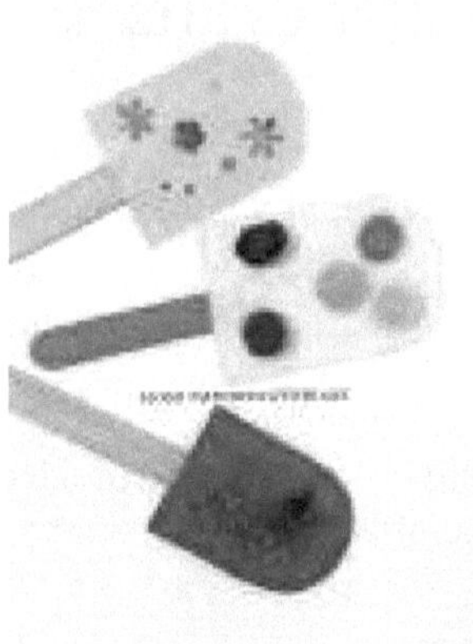

Frozen Toys

Summers are perfect time for playing with water and ice. Any child would love to see Frozen toys and then breaking the ice to excavate the toys.

Material Required:

- Toys
- Water
- Food color
- Plastic hammer or spoon

Well freezing the toys is easy part. Either freeze directly in a plastic box or use balloon for freezing the toy.

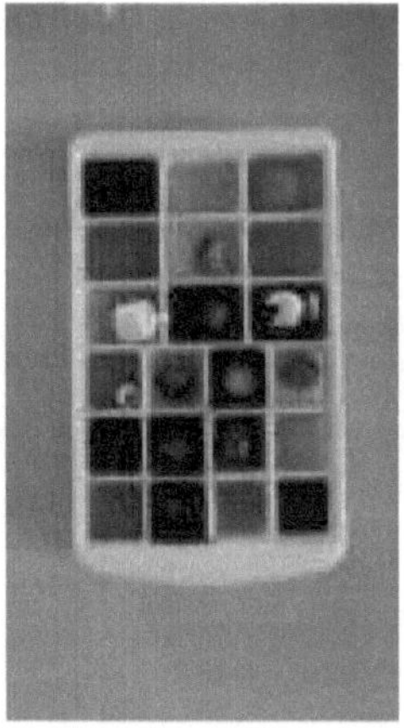

Add food color for more fun. *Excavating dinosaur fossils* has been our favorite.

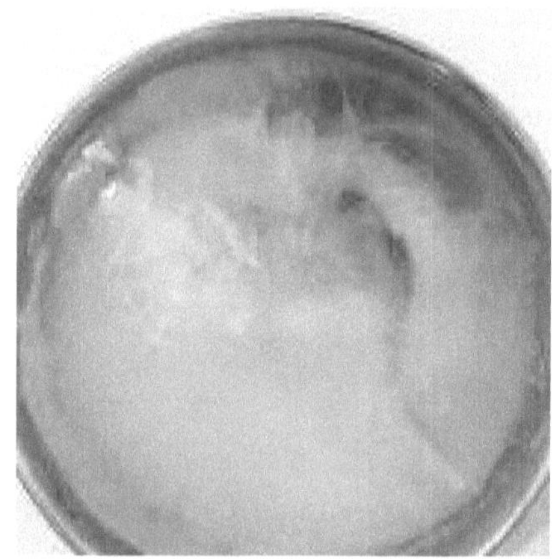

The fun part is breaking the ice or melting the ice. So we can use **3 techniques for exploring the frozen toy-**

- Breaking the ice with hammer or spoon
- Throwing the ice cubes in bath tub
- Pouring salt or warm water over ice

Some other interesting **water activities for summers** are:

- Paint the bath tub
- Spray paint
- Sink and float
- Bubble art
- Bubble bath for toys
- Salt Art

Also read Summer Activities for kids

Also read How to make Summer Vacations useful

Tree Crafts

TREES are depiction of seasons. Spring would have green lush leaves swinging on the trees, which began to turn yellow and fall in the autumn season. Winter is marked by the Christmas Tree all over the world.

So to teach kids about different seasons, trees are the best crafts to make with them. For the trees crafts, I have predominantly used **bubble wrap, straw and q-tips.** Use of these materials also has more benefits than just another craft activity:

- Fine motor skills
- Hand-eye coordination
- Cognitive skills
- Sensory skills
- Strengthening of hand muscles
- Creativity

These easy crafts are perfectly for Montessori curriculum or just following some absolutely practical Montessori teaching techniques at home.

Painting with Bubble Wrap
Material Required:

- Paint – green, yellow, red, orange, brown
- Bubble Wrap
- Brush

EVERGREEN TREE

Step 1: Draw a tree trunk and branches with brown color on white paper – use sketch colors or water colors

Step 2: Take green color on a plate and cut small pieces of bubble wrap

Step 3: Dip the bubble wrap in green color dab on the paper

Step 4: Now take yellow color near the green on the plate and mix little yellow with green. So now we have three shades – green, light green and yellow.

Step 5: Dab some leaves on ground too

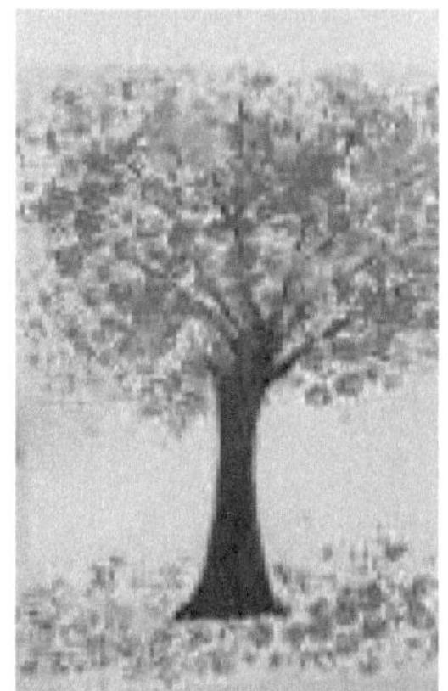

CHRISTMAS TREE

Step 1: Draw shape of a Christmas Tree on the white plain paper and paint brown tree trunk

Step 2: Use above steps to create tree but be careful of the shape.

Step 3: Paint ornaments of the tree with *finger-painting* – more fun for kids and sensory skills development

Step 4: Draw or stick a star on top of the tree

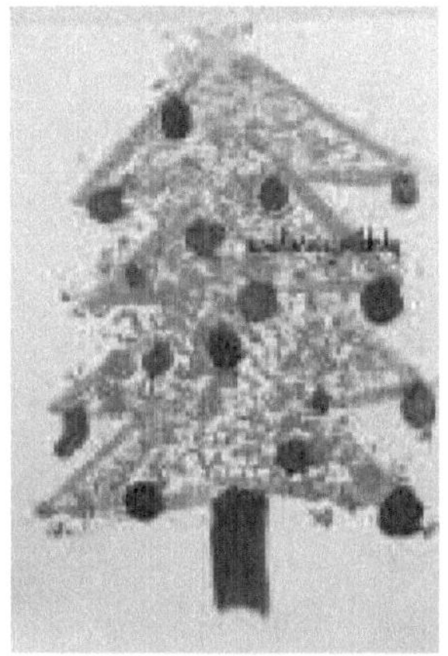

Check** Fall Trees **under Fall Crafts

Underwater Crafts

Underwater world is so beautiful and fascinating. The sight of colorful fish, jelly fish, star fish, green lush flora is absolutely amazing.

I believe all kids are amused by under the sea world and every child loves sea creatures. Be it jelly fish, octopus, crab, shark or just a golden fish. **Benefits of crafting with kids:**

- Enhances creativity
- Understanding of living creatures and body party
- Development of fine motor skills
- Cognitive development
- Language development
- Boosts bonding between child and caregiver

So here are some of the **Under the Sea Craft Ideas.**

Under the Sea World

This is a perfect recycle craft to put a show box to use and create a underwater world in your house. The paintings on the sides of the box are painted by the child and so are the fish, octopus, sea horse. Stuck them to the roof of the box and we have our sea-world ready.

Swimming Jelly Fish

This swimming Jelly Fish Craft is one of our most loved and viewed craft on Facebook. The jelly fish is made of felt with strands of colorful yarn as tentacles. Check step-by-step tutorial *here*. Or under Swimming Jelly Fish chapter.

Tissue Roll Octopus

I love reusing water items and hoard tissue rolls and tissue boxes so that I can always turn them into crafts and recycle. Absolutely simple and easy craft that 3 year old child can make. Check detailed steps for this tissue roll octopus *here*. Or under Tissue Roll Octopus chapter.

Why waste when you can DIY?

Paper Plate Fish

We love paper plates and the *paper plate crafts*. We have made masks, dinosaurs, owl etc from paper plates. These super easy paper plate fish crafts were a hit with my toddler that we ended up making two.

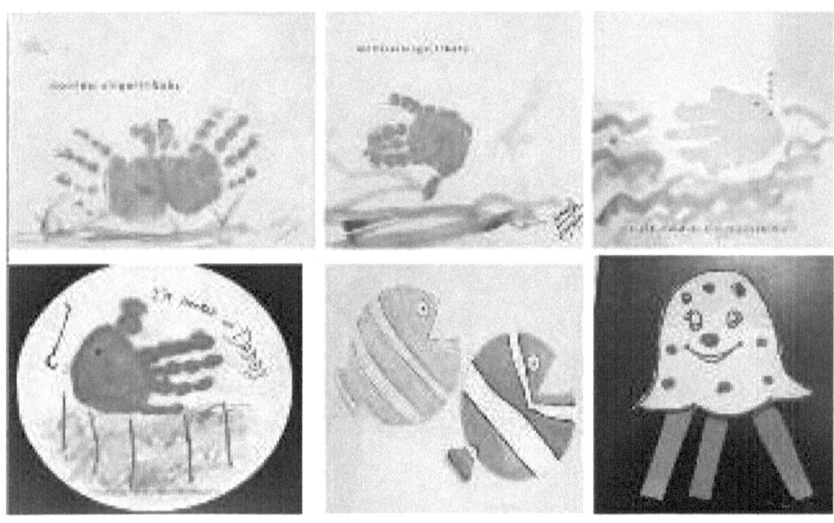

Handprint/Footprint Crafts

Why should we leave those tiny toddlers from enjoying crafting! Handprint and footprints crafts are the best for them. We can create fish, Crab, Octopus, Jelly fish by putting colors on those tiny hands.

TIP: Show the child how to put hands on the paper. Always use child-safe paints and keep tissues our cloth nearby and immediately wipe off the hands/foot.

Felt Fish

Felt quiet book are beneficial in helping kids develop their *fine and gross motor skills along with sensory skills*. The best part of using felt activity books are that they are *reusable, washable, and tear-proof*. Check step-by-step tutorial of no-sew felt quiet book *here* or **under No Sew Quiet Book**.

The Very Hungry Caterpillar Craft

The Very Hungry Caterpillar ate 1 apple, 2 pears, 3 plums, 4 strawberries, 5 oranges, and then he ate 1 cake slice, an icecream cone, a pickle, cherry pie, cheese, watermelon …. and he ate it all…. and then had a stomachache.

….. based on the book by **Eric Carle**.

This book is quite popular among young kids and educators. And it is available in various versions from board books to buggy books. Along with just reading the book, it's proven that associated crafts and activities increase interest in books along with other skill developments like *cognitive, language and social.*
This book also includes ***life cycle of caterpillar –***

Egg – Caterpillar – Cocoon – Butterfly

A lot of **activities** can be based on this children book from making paper caterpillar to PomPom caterpillar to butterfly and the whole life cycle or the weekdays fruits eating activity.

Paper Caterpillar
Here is a basic simple **Paper Caterpillar Craft** that can wriggle around by blowing with a straw.

Activity: Blowing Paper Caterpillar Craft with a Straw

This fun activity will keep kids busy for hours as they would love to feed the caterpillar all the food they can get their hands on. So since we love cooking pretend play and shopping play, we had a lot of fruits, vegetables, at our dispersal. However, in case you don't have plastic food toys, you can draw the fruits and vegetables on paper and use or use pictures.

Material Required:

- Colored paper
- Scissors
- Marker
- Straw
- Plastic food items or draw on paper or flash cards or pictures of food

Step 1: Cut a rectangular strip from the colored paper

Step 2: Fold the paper as shown in this _video_

Step 3: Mark it's face and we also drew a star on it's tail

Step 4: Now just keep blowing the caterpillar with straw to feed it on the food.

More Activities based on The Very Hungry Caterpillar Book:

- Life-cycle of Caterpillar
- Days of week
- Numbers and colors
- Feeding a caterpillar

It is proven that associating books with crafts and involving activities always have longer lasting impression on kids and are beneficial in many including *imagination, cognitive & language development.*

Winter Crafts

What does WINTER remind you of?

Ask this question to kids, and the first answer will be SNOWMAN. Well! I love snowman too.

So how about making a Snowman craft to get the cold winter season feeling.

I just love how flexible snowman is and it's so easy to be made. Since we don't live in snow area, we get the feel by making snowman crafts.

Snowman Craft for Kids:
The paper snowman Craft is an easy Peasy cute craft to do with young kids.

Material Required:

- Plain white paper
- Colors
- Glue
- Scissors
- Ribbon

Step 1: Cut the paper in the shape of snowman and it's hat

Step 2: Stick it together and Color it

Step 3: Stick a coloful ribbon or cloth or felt scarf for adding zing.

This was super easy cutest no-sew Craft I have ever tried.

Material Required:

- Old white socks
- Grains/Rice
- Googly eyes
- Pompom
- Ribbon
- Red Felt
- Buttons

Step 1: Fill the grains/rice in the sock – 3/4 level

Step 2: Tie with a rubber band at the top and also in between to make face and body

Step 3: Turn the upper opening part upside down to make it's cap

Step 4: Tie ribbon on the neck

Step 5: Stick googly eyes and felt nose

Step 6: Stick buttons and PomPom on head

No-sew Snowman is ready to roll!!.

X-Mas Crafts & Activities

Xmas or Christmas is that time of the year when the whole world is filled with happiness and excitement and hope of celebrating the festival with the loved ones. The time of the year when people look forward to meeting families and friends and reunite.

What could be better way of celebrating Christmas than doing some pretty crafts and interesting activities with kids! Festivals are best occasions to start some family rituals.

Kids can also be encouraged to make _**hand-made gifts**_ and _**Greetings cards**_ to present to friends, family and teachers.

Christmas Tree Felt Craft

Making a _**felt Xmas Tree**_ with felt can be reused every year again and again and gives so many options of decorating your own tree.. perfect for any child.

Material Required:

- Felt
- Scissors
- Markers
- Pompoms
- Stars, jewel
- Glue

So each time the child can decorate his own personal Christmas Tree as per his own wish, no one to object him. Bet it would be exhilarating for little kids.

Coloring a Christmas Tree is bit common but painting the same tree with a twist would be more fun, isn't it !
So try coloring a Christmas Tree using bubble wrap. Check step-by-step guide _here_. Or under Tree Crafts.

Popsicle Reindeer Craft

What is a Christmas without Reindeer!
So let's make a cute Popsicle reindeer and hang it on the Christmas tree or around the house for Christmas decoration.
Google eyes and red PomPom nose added character to it, right!

Wait starting to decorate till the stuck popsicles dry completely.

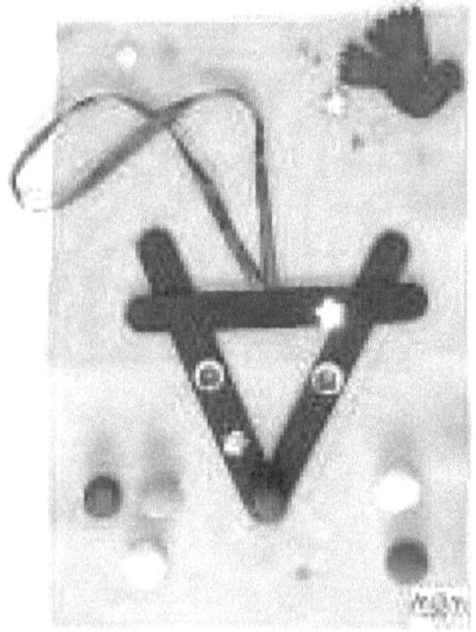

It can be used a cute hand-made Christmas gift for friends/teachers/neighbors.

Angel Craft

Let's make some angels to add more positivity and hope to our Christmas decor and crafts gallery with a cloth-pin angel with felt wings and PomPom face and little golden glitter glue on it.

Material Required:

- Clothes-pin
- Glue
- White felt or paper for wings
- White Pompom for face
- Marker
- Golden glitter or glitter glue
- Ribbon for halo

It is easy to make. Just stick pompom head, felt or paper wings, a ribbon halo and some glitter.

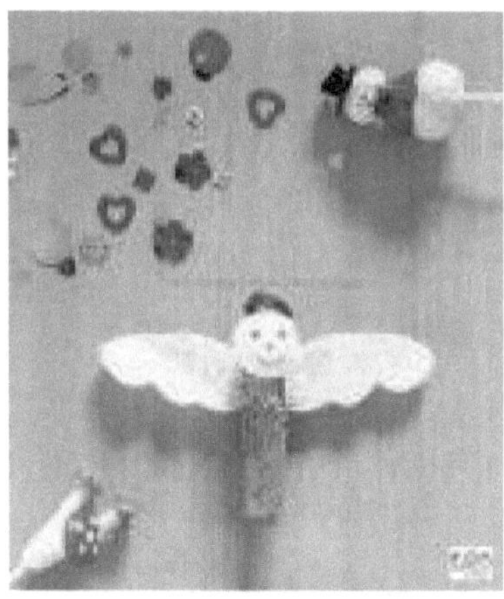

Yarn Crafts

Yarn Crafts are our recent discovered love and we are totally loving making Pompoms with yarn and little one helps in making Pompoms and then enjoy playing with them.

I just got few left over Yarn bundles remaining from my mom's work. The colors availability in yarn gives lot of scope for variety and creativity. We have made PomPom birdies, Jelly fish, cat and bunny so far using yarns.

Mommy & Baby Yarn PomPom birdie

It's easier than I thought to make Pompoms with yarn, even my 5 year old helped out in making these **DIY Yarn PomPoms.**

Material Required:

- Yarn
- Scissors
- Fork
- Googly eyes
- Red paper
- Glue

Step 1: Using the usual technique of making PomPom with a fork – tie the yarn around the fork and take multiple rounds according to the size you want – we made 2 sizes for mommy and baby birdie.

Step 2: Then tie from center and take out from the fork and cut the edges and give the symmetry

Step 3: Fluff the Pompom by rubbing in between palm

Step 4: Stick google eyes and red nose

Cute, isn't it! The eyes just added life to the PomPom balls.
The little boy was super proud of himself and so we made two of these Yarn PomPom birdies.
See a short _**stop-motion video**_ we made.

Yarn Cat/ Kitten

So I have used similar technique as above for Pompms, except I have used fingers instead of fork.

Material Required:

- Yarn
- Scissors
- Googly eyes
- Glue
- Foam / felt

Steps are same as above PomPom birdies, except I used finger to make this, didn't take that any rounds and didn't cut the edges too short. So left the yarn as a flattened disc type shape.

Then stuck googly eyes, foam ears and nose and black yarn whiskers.I have used a multi-colored yarn, nay color yarn can be used for making cat.

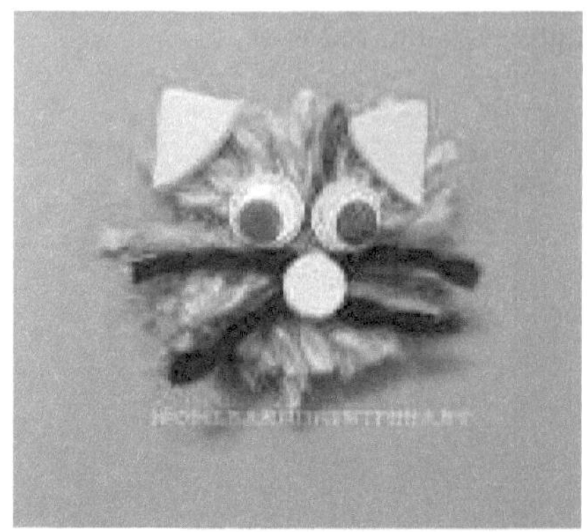

Yarn Rabbit/ Bunny

Exactly the same steps as the yarn kitty above. I have Just changed the shape of its foam ears. I found using fingers was easier for quicker Crafts when we are taking lesser yarn rounds.

Do they look like siblings? LOL

The similar Looking furry cuties right! To much difference except the long bunny ears and short kitty ears – both are swift and fast.

Zoo Animal Crafts

Zoo is the most loved place that every child wants to visit and kids' affection for animals is obvious. Making animal crafts is all time favorite and I think I have not met any child till date who doesn't like animals – be it wild or domestic or farm animals.

Animal crafts offer so much variety and easy to make with paper or paper plates or tissue rolls or cardboard boxes or just handprint and footprint. And we have tried a lot of them. One can practically create crafts with all the zoo animals.

Since we can't go to the zoo at the moment, let's make craft a zoo craft at home.

Paper Zoo Craft
Absolutely easy to make a paper zoo and super fun.

Material Required:

- White paper sheet
- Colors
- Yarn threads
- Glue
- Animal stickers or drawn on paper

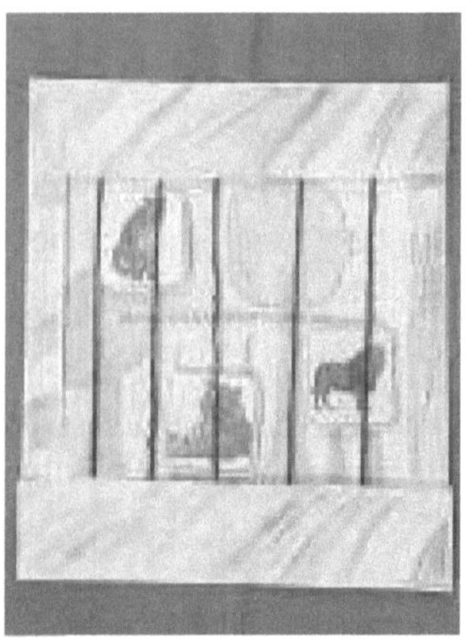

Step 1: Fold the sheet of paper from all 4 sides, as shown in picture

Step 2: Draw and color trees, grass, sky and the zoo frame as per choice. We made a multicolored zoo

Step 3: Fold small pieces of paper multiple times and stick One side on base paper and Other side on the animal picture (ref pic above and below) – gives 3D effect to the zoo

Step 4: Stick pieces of black yarn or thread from top to bottom as shown above and also stick a folded paper each side to give 3D effect

See more **Zoo Animal Crafts**